i found god in my hair

98 spiritual principles I learned... from my hair!

Tanya Wright

thank you

Nicole Wood
Lisa O'Brien
Wil Colom
Marco Armantini
Kaaryn Simmons
Jennifer DaSilva
Alexandra Rizio
Cheri Bessellieu
Erik Ping Wang
Matt Farrell
Roberto Alfarez
My family
Start Small, Think Big
Columbia Small Business Development Program
Weil, Gotshal
Simpson, Thacher
The Sundance Institute's New Frontier Lab

My mother

dedication

This book is dedicated to anyone and everyone in the history of the universe who has ever struggled with their hair!

...and a special shout out goes to the women (and men!) around the world with textured hair, bloggers and the YouTube Natural Hair Community, for whom I have great gratitude and from who I draw tremendous inspiration.

The ancient civilizations used to say that our thoughts dwelled in our hair. It has a biologic function, but we ornament it, giving it a social meaning. Hair is a message—it's a message we give to the world about our personality. The hair is the protection of our skin, the memory throughout centuries of our body and our social message. Within its chemistry, hair keeps our mood and the memory of our ailments. Hair is the most indestructible part of our organism. Maybe in a thousand years, somebody can take a look at our hair and know something about us.

— thehistoryofthehairsworld.com

foreword

I had some trouble with the title of this book.

For many, "God" is a very loaded word. I get it. I grappled with changing the title for fear that I might alienate people, especially the ones that were too cool, too smart or simply didn't believe in God. Trust me, I've gone through my own rocky relationship with the man (or woman?) upstairs. I went round and round on this and came back to my first choice title, mostly because it was true.

This book is about the things I learned about life via my relationship with what has been the bane of my existence for most of my existence: MY HAIR! I was responsible for putting the physical time, research and energy into the book, but the inspiration to write it—the thing that kept goading me forward—is something (or someone) I can't fully explain. Also inside are fun quotes by some folks you know and love, plus photos of my various roles as an actress and all my hairstyles along the way. I wrote these essays long before I got the role of hairdresser Crystal Burset on the Netflix original series ORANGE IS THE NEW BLACK. What a happy coincidence!

And yes, I believe there is a God. Some people call it the Universe. Others call it energy. Or Yahweh. And then there's Jesus! Jehovah is another choice and so is Allah. Although I'm a writer, this word—God— is so loaded for most people, I thought it best to stay away from it completely. But there are reams of scientists who acknowledge that there are some things that cannot be explained and credit some unknown source many describe simply as "other"—including Einstein, the most famous scientist of them all.

I can certainly tell you what this book is not: a socio-political manifesto on the merits of whether one wears their hair natural or relaxed, braided or weaved, cut or colored. There are enough people talking about that sorta stuff, and I just ain't one of them. This is a book that, I hope, will inspire health and wellness no matter which style you choose to wear your hair.

One last note: your mind will want to believe that some precepts in this book are redundant (for example, the words "thank you" and "gratitude"). But there are subtle and profound differences—you'll understand once you start reading...

Whether you believe there is a God or not, I hope you'll find the precepts in this book useful to your life and apply them. Some people find God in a church, art, their children or their animals. Me? Well, I found God in the most unlikeliest of places: I Found God in My Hair.

one: infinite possibilities

I am a dreamer—for sure. But dreams rarely become a reality until you take action. I am an obsessive finisher and terribly, terribly determined—perhaps it's the Taurus in me! Once I get a goal fixed in my mind, I rarely veer off course until I have achieved it, no matter how large the task.

Here's the thing: I believe that one of the prerequisites of dreaming is that you have to believe that what you dream is possible in order for it to become true! And the truth is anything is possible! The world is made up of infinite possibilities.

Our hair is made up of millions of hair follicles, too; follicles are CIRCULAR in shape, like the letter "o" or the number 0. According to the dictionary, this shape is also representative of "pure potentiality;" it is also the "number from which all numbers spring forth." In essence, we have thousands and thousands of "o's" atop our head.

My hair is a reminder that I have infinite possibilities at my disposal.

two: patience

Length is a popular desire among most women with textured hair—who doesn't want a long, luxurious mane? But growing your hair requires patience—length just doesn't happen overnight. When you see a gal with long, flowing coifs you can be sure that it took a while to get it there.

For me, patience is the "trait most desired." Whenever I feel myself getting impatient, I instinctively switch my thoughts to the present moment and start breathing—whatever it is I'm waiting for invariably comes without me being stressed and pressed about it and often when I'm not looking at all. I does feel like "a watched pot never boils."

My hair journey has been very long and extremely windy. My hair teaches me to have patience.

three:
indestructible

Did you know that our hair is the most indestructible part of our bodies? It contains our DNA—that's pretty strong! Sometimes we get swept to and fro by the tide of life—we are happy when we have 'good' days, and not-so-much when we have 'bad' ones. There is a part in all of us that isn't swept by the tide, no matter what our external world looks like, no matter what changes in fortune for us.

My hair teaches me that, no matter what I may experience in the external world, that I am indestructible.

four: elasticity

Ah, curls! I have lots of them, all over my head. Springy coils that swing to my shoulders when wet and shrink up toward my scalp when they're dry. I can pull a curl taut and release it and it snaps back—like a rubber band. Life is full of changes, so sometimes, I have to change direction, chart another course. This has happened to me more times than I care to count!

My hair teaches me to be elastic so that I can deal with whatever twists and turns life throws at me.

"People always ask me how long it takes to do my hair. I don't know, I'm never there."

— Dolly Parton

five: versatility

People tell me all the time I'm a chameleon—I can look very different from one day to the next. The truth is, my look—what I wear, how I wear my hair— depends largely on how I feel when I wake up in the morning. I am an actress so my profession demands that I be versatile, but in life, I have found it's good to be versatile, too. The ability to relate to different kinds of people—to move from one group to the next and have something in common with all of them—is a sign of a versatile person.

My hair teaches me to be versatile.

six: control

My hair journey started from one simple idea: "if I could get control of my hair, maybe—just maybe—I can get control of my life!" My professional life is always changing—it's unpredictable! It's hard to plan things in advance because the circumstances of my life can change on a dime—and often have. Before I read the book "Curly Like Me" (a great book for women with naturally textured hair written by Teri LaFleur), I had resigned myself to the fact that my hair was just something I would not be able to control— ever. 'Curly Like Me' gave me hope; it helped me to see that there WAS a method to the madness, and there WAS a way to deal with my hair where I was in control of it instead of feeling like it was always in control of me.

My hair teaches me that I have control.

"It's the way we treat the hair once it's on top of our heads that literally makes it or breaks it."

— Unknown

seven: attachment

"My hair is like a box of chocolates: I never know what I'm gonna get." Rather than get attached to the result of something—of thinking that things should look and be a way that they aren't—I have learned not to get attached to a fixed picture in my mind. Letting go of attachment is, perhaps, one of the most profound life lessons I've ever learned. Almost all of the world's spiritual teachers say that attachment most often leads to misery.

My hair has taught me to detach myself from results.

eight: tolerance

I have curly textured hair. My hair will NEVER grow out of my head in any other way that it grows now. EVER. I accept that now, but it wasn't easy getting here. First, I had to tolerate it, including tolerating awkward lengths for a year or so after I did the "Big Chop." Now, when I have to endure something I don't like, I can tolerate it better (usually by breathing and slowing down my mind.)

My hair has taught me to be more tolerant.

nine: kindness

I was so frustrated with my curls for most of my life! For years, I would rake a dry comb through my fragile hair strands, just hoping to create some order out of what I thought was the most profound chaos. My hair would snap, crackle and pop under the pressure— I was not being kind to my curls.

My hair has taught me to be kind. Kind to others, but mostly to myself.

ten: nurture

When I take the time to nurture my hair, I feel good about myself. I'm a bit of a workaholic and, at times, I'll just go-go-go without resting at all in between, without nurturing myself. After experiencing burn out, I learned the importance of nurturing and taking care of myself— before anyone or anything. When I'm being good to my hair, I'm being good to myself.

My hair has taught me that nurturing myself regularly is vital to my happiness.

"She was the most beautiful creature on Earth - her hair said so in that language only hair can speak."

— Gabriel Bá, *Daytripper*

eleven: love

Love. It is the simplest of the four-letter words, but I believe it's also the one with the most impact. We throw the word "love" around a lot, but do we really know what it means? I'm reminded of the quote on love from the Bible: "Love is patient, love is kind..." This is the word that embodies all others in this book. There have been times in my life where I thought I was "in love" but was astounded by the quickness in which I could walk away from a grievous situation. Same with my hair—I can't tell you how many days I've thrown my hands up in frustration! But my hair grows out of my head—I am forever wedded to it. It's not something I can simply "walk away from" and, after some time, I had to choose to love it. If you have not love, what do you have?

My hair has taught me to love myself and others. Love them better. Love them faster. And love them stronger.

THE COSBY SHOW (NBC)

My first audition–and first job–was playing Theo's girl-friend on The Cosby Show. Now, aside from the fact that my eyebrows took over most my face, people still recognize me as "Tanya Simpson" to this day! As you can see, the hair stylist made her (and my!) life simple by simply putting "The Great Bush" that is my hair into one inverted cornrow down the side of my head. Tanya and Theo (played by Malcolm-Jamal Warner) shared their first onscreen kiss in this episode. He gave me a fake diamond ring for $19.95!

twelve: persistence

Ah, yes! Persistence—it's simply impossible to reach any goal without this little handy-dandy trait, whether it's with your hair or your life. I've gotta be honest, I struggle with this one a lot. It's not in me to "give up," but it's easy to get pretty discouraged when you've tried and tried and tried and tried...but sometimes, it just takes trying one. More. Time! Other times, it takes shifting your sights or efforts in another direction. Sometimes it means even being a pest! I've noticed that people who don't take no for an answer are most always the ones who eventually get what they want.

There were days when, no, I didn't want to work through my issues with my hair. But I focused on the goal a lot to get me through the tough times, times when I just wanted to give up. Persistence has helped me achieve the results I want, and has been invaluable in goal setting.

My hair has helped me to be more persistent.

THE COSBY SHOW (NBC)

...and, just as quickly, Tanya and Theo break up: in the episode "Man Talk," he thinks he's letting me down easy, but I beat him to the punch–I have a crush on a fella named Charlie Meyers. As you can see, "The Great Bush" was in full effect–AGAIN! This was shot about an hour after my hair was completely blow-dried straight–as you can see, it's as poofy as can be. Should have been my first indication that my hair just wanted to "be"...

thirteen: resilient

When I was 12, my mother took my sister and I to a beauty school in the Bronx to get our hair done. We didn't have much money, but she wanted us to learn about being good to ourselves as young women and a beauty school was what she could afford. I walked into the school with shoulder length hair and, when I walked out, I had something resembling a buzz cut. I'll never forget jumping out of the chair in tears—with the plastic cape still around my neck—and running across the street to my mother. She wiped my tears away and told me that my hair would grow back: that statement stopped my tears in its tracks. That's the thing about hair: unless you have an illness or take medication—and even in those instances—hair almost always grows back. So, no need to fret! Just wait it out and enjoy rocking what you have in the meantime.

Life doesn't always go as planned, but it's all about what you do in the moment AFTER it kicks you in the butt and brings you to your knees. I bounced back quick that day, and never cried about cut hair again.

My hair has taught me to be resilient.

"My hair had grown out long and shaggy—not in that sexy-young-rock-star kind of way but in that time-to-take-Rover-to-the-groomer kind of way."

— Jim Butcher, White Night

fourteen: damage

Sometimes in love, some people stay much longer than they should. They've been unhappy for some time—with no resolution in sight—but they stay out of sheer habit. It reminds me of a split end—if you cut it, you won't have the immediate "desired length," but...won't it cause more damage in the long run if it stays around?

Sometimes, it's best to cut things off—people, circumstances—in your life and start anew. Holding on to something that is damaging to your soul or psyche isn't good or healthy.

My hair has taught me to let go of things—and people— who are otherwise damaging to prevent further damage. Letting go also accelerates the growth process because, by cutting off the "bad stuff" now, you've immediately said "yes" to making a way for the good stuff.

My hair teaches me that damage can be damaging and helps me to let go.

MAMA FLORA'S FAMILY (CBS)

Ah, one of my favorite projects: Mama Flora's Family oppo-
site Cicely Tyson, Queen Latifah and Blair Underwood.
This was the last of famed writer Alex Haley's series of
books. We shot this in Georgia. I played a sweet country
girl named Ernestine (Blair's wife), where I aged from
15-37. This is, mostly, my hair with the help of custom
made extensions from the best place on the planet for
add-on hair: Extensions Plus. They're kinda pricey but
if you want to have a versatile look and have your hair
color/ texture matched to a T, these folks are the best in
the business–and I ain't getting paid to say it! Here are
a few of my period hairstyles from Mama Flora's Family.

MAMA FLORA'S FAMILY (CBS)

fifteen: protection

This is a biggie! I find my hair thrives the most when it is protected—either by styling (twists, buns) or silk scarves at night. Whenever it is kept in hibernation (and I usually do this if I'm working from home and/or puttering around the house), it's protected from the elements of heat or cold, both of which can be damaging to the hair.

Be mindful of when you need to protect yourself. Now, I'm not saying go out in the world and be fearful of everyone and everything you encounter—on the contrary. Danger is real, and arming yourself with protection in any endeavor can make you even more fearless as you pursue whatever goal you set out for yourself.

My hair has taught me the importance of protecting myself as I fearlessly navigate life.

"I think that the most important thing a woman can have — next to talent, of course — is her hairdresser."

— Joan Crawford

sixteen: retention

There's merit in wanting to retain what you've worked hard for. Whether it's your marriage...or your hair! For example, in marriage, it's best to weave in a steady stream of honest communication if you want to retain a healthy, balanced and long-lasting relationship. I've seen this work wonders in my life— there are no "assumptions" about things, and usually when you talk about the "hard stuff" early on and right off the bat, it leaves more time for play! I see hair in the same way. There are things I do constantly to my hair (i.e., protective styles, keeping it moisturized, etc.) that help to retain its length, luster, shine and basic overall health.

My hair has taught me how to retain the things in my life that I value.

"Gray hair is God's graffiti."

— Bill Cosby

seventeen: shedding

It's the most natural of processes. We are constantly shedding skin and hair, all day every day. It's not always visible, but the body knows this is a healthy process of any living organism. Shedding is nature's way of slough-ing off the old and making way for the new! I used to be so devastated after the end of a relationship when I was younger— now, as I've gotten older (and hopefully wiser!) there's little if any pain related to shedding, whether it's my hair, a relationship or circumstance.

My hair has taught me to receive shedding with grace. 'Cause you never know what's on the other side...

eighteen: stretch

My hair is CURL-LY!! I mean, crazy curly! I've learned to keep my hair stretched as much as I can so it doesn't curl back into itself—if I don't, I get these tiny knots that form at the ends. I usually band my hair at night so the curls are lengthened which prevents these "fairy knots" from forming. I also know that the more I stretch my body and mind—yoga is great for this, especially when I am deep in thought or trying to work something out in my mind— the more I'm able to make space for an answer. Stretching takes the rust off and keeps you pliable for sure!

My hair has taught me the importance of constant, everyday stretching.

WANTED: DEAD OR ALIVE, "RAPUNZEL"
For horse thieving, kidnapping, jail breaking, and using her hair in a manner other than nature intended!
— Shannon Hale, Rapunzel's Revenge

nineteen: conflict

Most people avoid it, and some brave souls go boldly toward it. Dealing with conflict is an indicator that something's not working at its optimum, giving you the opportunity to make changes. Most people want to see change in their life, but they don't want to BE the change.

It was the conflict between me and my hair that urged me to go down the rabbit hole of writing this collection of essays! Conflict can be a good thing if you're willing to investigate and do the work to make the changes to improve things for yourself.

My hair teaches me how to embrace conflict in my life.

"I am not my hair, I am not this skin, I am not your expectations / I am not my hair, I am not this skin, I am the soul that lives within."

— India Arie, I AM NOT MY HAIR

twenty: change

Change is one of the few things that we can rely on experiencing as long as we're alive. Many fight it, but why fight the inevitable? Our bodies are changing—time is passing—and it would be unwise to forever think we will always be the same.

The same has been true for my hair: I've fried it, dyed it, laid it to the side, weaved it, braided it, you name it! I've changed my hair any number of ways, depending on my mood. Changing it can be fun.

My hair has helped me to not only embrace change but to celebrate it each time it shows up in my life!

twenty-one: courage

Hair—particularly in the African-American community— has oft been fodder for political expression. Diatribes on the merits of straightening or not, weaving or not, natural or not have been written by many, many people. The truth is, most people don't have the courage to be themselves— whatever that is. Most folks follow the herd.

I started to wear my hair natural because I was interested, simply, in wearing it the way it actually grew out of my head. It wasn't a political statement. I never cared too much about what people thought of me (I learned early you can't please everybody) and I sure wasn't going to start now.

My hair taught me to have courage to be who I truly am, even if it looks different from everyone else around me.

twenty-two: fragility

I have very, very, very fine hair—it's extremely fragile, so it's no wonder it snapped off when I raked the dryer over it or neglected to moisturize it for a day or more. Some heads can withstand more than others, but I know that my hair can't. And I honor that.

My hair taught me to respect fragility with tenderness whenever and wherever I find it.

"Hair on a man's chest is thought to denote strength. The gorilla is the most powerful of bipeds and has hair on every place on his body except for his chest."

— Anton Szandor LaVey

twenty-three: practice

A few years ago, I noticed that people started asking me questions about my hair. "What do you put in it? How do you get it to curl up like that?" The truth is, for most of my life, my hair was my biggest thorn and I ain't ashamed to say it was a hot mess.

Nothing gets great on its own nor does it suddenly improve overnight. A prima ballerina spends endless hours in rehearsal to get her plies just right; master cellists rehearse unceasingly to learn how to hit just the right notes at the right time. I can't tell you how many drafts of screenplays I've written over the years just to eek something out I felt was worthwhile for human eyes. Folks usually don't see the blood, sweat and tears you put into something, just the result of your blood, sweat and tears.

I was determined to master my hair, and so I did what I always did when I want to get better at something— I practiced. Try practicing something you want to master when other folks are watching TV or playing video games. You might not be the life of the party but, in time, you'll find you've reached your goal—whatever that may be.

My hair teaches me every day that practice makes perfect.

"We'll probably never save our souls — but hell, at least we'll get our hair sorted."
— Siddharth Dhanvant Shanghvi,
The Last Song of Dusk: A Novel

twenty-four: assistance

I cannot tell you how grateful I am for the ladies on YouTube. WOW! Hundreds of women have posted videos about All Things Hair and they have helped me so so very much! Their assistance has been invaluable as I transitioned my relaxed hair to its natural state.

My hair teaches me to seek and ask for assistance when I need it. No man— or woman— is an island!

twenty-five:
nature

When times were lean and mean in my very early days as an actress and I couldn't afford hair conditioner, I went to my kitchen! Mayo. Egg. Avocado. Olive Oil. Coconut Milk. Shea Butter. The natural stuff was accessible, had great value and often did a better job than the highly processed stuff. I made these hair pastes my weekly ritual, spending time with myself, pouring myself a glass of sparkling apple cider (I don't drink) and taking a load off while God's Harvest did the heavy lifting on my hair.

My hair teaches me to enjoy nature's bounty and that what works for the inside also works for the outside.

twenty-six: faith

Without it, there's nothing. You can work as hard as you want, read every book in the world, do all the things you see other "successful" people doing, but without faith you're just spinning your wheels.

It took a while for my hair to get on track. Many times I just wanted to quit and slap some relaxer on it. I didn't always know where I was going— and, I'll confess, I didn't always feel great about the journey—but I had faith that I was headed in the right direction.

I have questioned my faith more times than I can count. The thing about faith, I realized, is that you have to let go of "how" something is going to happen and just fix your mind on "that" it's going to happen—or, better yet, embrace the fact that it's already happening!

It's a hard one to truly master, but there are few things more powerful than faith. Period.

My hair teaches me to have faith!

twenty-seven: community

If I'm not careful, I can be a hermit. I can spend days or weeks in the solace of my home and mind, creating worlds on paper and conceiving characters that live. The importance of community, though, can never be underestimated.

When I found there was a vibrant textured hair community online, I was so excited! There was so much to learn, to share, to exchange. I felt like the community was something bigger than myself, something that I could both feed from and contribute to.

My hair taught me the importance of community as an anchor and ever-present well of inspiration in my life.

"If I want to knock a story off the front page, I just change my hairstyle."

— Hillary Rodham Clinton

twenty-eight:
uniqueness

Hair is like a fingerprint: no two heads are exactly the same. There are, literally, a billion ways to express your thoughts, feelings and emotions through your hair. Our hair gives us an opportunity every day to celebrate our own uniqueness.

My hair reminds me that I am a unique being and I have the ability to express myself in any way I want through it.

THE BROTHERS (Screen Gems)

This was a short bit in the urban comedy, The Brothers; I played a woman named LaMuzindah. I only had one scene in this movie and I was determined to be remembered: I ornamented my VERY "be-weavable" hair with a big, bold white flower! This was a fun scene:) One day while I was in the Department of Motor Vehicles renewing my license, a lady walked up to me and quoted this entire scene word for word!

twenty-nine: freedom

There are many words to describe my hair and "free" is definitely one of them! When my hair is loose and completely unencumbered is when I feel most like myself, it's when I feel the most free! When it's in its wildest, craziest state is when, strangely, I feel most relaxed.

Freedom has been a recurring theme in my life. A friend told me years ago that the reason I wasn't married was because I valued my freedom too much. Dunno if that's true or not— I know some married people who seem incredibly free–but there might be something to explore here. Maybe the statement that "freedom is more a state of mind" is accurate.

My hair teaches me that I am forever free.

thirty: water

Most of the earth is covered in water; similarly, most of the body is made up of H2O. We can live without many things, but no one— no living thing— can live without water. This is a biggie. Every cell in our body needs it every moment of the day. They say dehydration is the root of countless health problems, and I really do believe that it's true.

You need water. Your body needs water.

I know that my hair—and every part of me—needs water in order to survive and to thrive.

thirty-one: play

I haven't been 10 years old in some time (LOL!), but my favorite hair style, hands down, are two power puff balls on either side of my head. I style my hair like this whenever I'm feeling playful.

My dog, Macarena, is a Labrador Retriever. And if any of you have or know anything at all about Labs, you know they love two things: water and balls! Macarena has made a religion out of placing a tennis ball in my lap whenever I feel life getting heavy, and this simple act immediately makes me smile and throw the ball, which is her ultimate goal.

My hair reminds me that I have the choice of how I'm going to respond to stressful situations in life. It reminds me there is always the choice to take the lighter load and that whenever I can, I should choose to play. Playing can change perspective.

thirty-two: sun

I stumbled on the Beatles' "Here Comes the Sun" while watching vloggers on YouTube—Nina Simone's version of the song is out of this world! A few months ago, my mother bought me a mirror that looks like the sun and I put it over my bed. This "sunny" mirror reminded me of my hair! The round shape was my face and my hair, the rays of the sun. The sun has always been a thing that has made me happy in my life. Its ever-present grace and benevolence sits high in the sky, the warmth and light making a way, rising daily and without fail.

My hair teaches me to never take the rising and the setting of the sun for granted. Every day is a new day and a new chance to start again. The sun makes me feel hopeful. I love the sun!

"I stared at her black hair. It was shiny like the promises in magazines."

— Alice Sebold, The Lovely Bones

thirty-three: beauty

Beauty is not an indulgence—I believe it actually inspires creativity. I'll never forget the time I was in Rome and went to the Vatican for the first time to witness the splendor that is the Sistine Chapel; the moments walking through the Brooklyn Botanical Gardens or watching the Alvin Ailey dancers perform their yearly Christmas-time triumph. It stirs something within me that urges me to create something that can only hope to complement the beauty I see before me.

But beauty is an inside job that manifests itself in an outward reality. When you feel beautiful, you tend to automatically look beautiful. The work I was doing on the "inner" me manifested itself in my outside me. Around the time I started to believe that my hair was "beautiful," I also began to drink more water and work out. Not to look beautiful, but because I already felt beautiful:)

My hair helped me to reveal the beauty I already felt inside.

thirty-four: grace

According to the dictionary, the word "grace" is defined as "elegance or beauty of form, manner, motion, or action." In action, grace is a way of moving that is smooth and attractive, not stiff or awkward. In spiritual terms, grace is the mercy given to us by God. Grace is one of my favorite words–the very sound of it makes me feel peaceful.

Well, it took a lot of work, practice, commitment and resilience to get here, but you can't tell me that my hair is not Grace in action:)

thirty-five: forgiveness

I got from being frustrated with my hair to downright loving it by forgiving—myself. I had to forgive myself for adopting ideas about my hair that belonged to other people—ideas that were not mine. They say "when you know better, you do better." I had to forgive myself for following the herd; forgive myself for trying to cover up, alter or otherwise change what grew out of my head to fit some societal idea.

My hair taught me that, before I forgive others for wrongs or perceived slights, I have to first forgive myself.

thirty-six: charity

It's good to be generous—actually, no—it's great to be generous! I have come to believe that the purpose of our lives on the planet is to help others. There is no greater work than giving, volunteering or being philanthropic. Those that give generally have no problems in life being taken care of by the universe.

But charity begins at home.

One of the great spiritual principles of money is that one must pay oneself first. This took a long time for me to adopt and accept–I always thought I should pay others first. You have to show the world—I dare say the universe— how you want to be treated. And in order to pay other people, you have to first get paid yourself— right?

I had to get right with myself via my hair so that I might endeavor to help you get right with yours. I had to give myself the things I hoped people would give to me one day. I can truly say that it works:)

My hair taught me to be more charitable to others by being charitable to myself.

Interviewer: "So Frank, you have long hair. Does that make you a woman?"

Frank Zappa: "You have a wooden leg. Does that make you a table?"

— Frank Zappa

thirty-seven: gratitude

Being grateful in the midst of perceived misfortune is extremely difficult. It's hard to see generosity in the face of earth-shattering, cataclysmic change. When my brother died some years ago, I thought I would die with him; in fact, I believe a part of me did.

The lessons he left in his wake were enormous. Gratitude is hard to cultivate when your heart is bust so wide open.

I never in a million years thought I would be writing a book about my hair! AH! My hair has been a thorn in my side ever since I could remember. But once I began to cultivate gratitude for it, it began to give back to me in ways I could have never imagined.

My hair teaches me how to be grateful for what I already have. And that what I have is beautiful–and enough!

"24" (FOX)

"24" Season 1! I remember the audition for this—it was the day after I shot another pilot that year. We shot that pilot until 6 AM and I had the audition for "24" at 10 AM! Needless to say, I was bleary-eyed and had very little energy. I was astounded when I found out I got the part! I played Senator Palmer's (Dennis Haysbert's) right hand gal Patty Brooks. The role of Patty was originally written for a man ("Nathaniel"), but was changed to a woman at the last minute. "24" was a heart pounding, ground-breaking, series — the title, the format (an entire season took place in 24 hours). Everything.

Now, there's a hairy story here: I wore a wig my first few episodes of "24" ; then, I decided to wear my own hair (which, as you can see below, is decidedly shorter). Since continuity is such a big deal with a show like this, the hair folks on the show were freaking out, but the Executive Producer loved my hair. "Why didn't you always wear your hair?" he asked. I didn't have an answer. I was just following the herd, I guess. Until I decided not to...

My "new" hair. In the same 24 hours! LOL! (FOX)

thirty-eight: volunteer

I spent the weekend with my friend Sarah; her daughter Maddy has hair with a similar texture to mine. When I arrived, the girl's hair had clearly not been combed in months—it was matted so bad it was starting to dread. They weren't like beautiful dreadlocks, just a hot matted mess of uncombed hair–very different. When I asked Sarah about Maddy's hair, she almost broke down in a heap of tears. Sarah was frustrated and ashamed about what to do with her little girl's mane. We went to the store and purchased some hair products; when we came back, I proceeded to show Sarah how to do Maddy's hair. Now, I admit this was not a fun time for little Maddy, but I promised next time would be better. And better, and better and better...

When we were done, Sarah thanked me profusely. There was no need, though —she was my friend and Maddy is practically my niece! I'd do whatever I could to help. It made me feel good to volunteer that day and I decided I was going to do more of it.

My hair helped me to realize how volunteering helps makes other people's lives better. And makes me feel great!

"Symbolic of life, hair bolts from our head[s]. Like the earth, it can be harvested, but it will rise again. We can change its color and texture when the mood strikes us, but in time it will return to its original form, just as Nature will in time turn our precisely laid-out cities into a weed-way."

— Diane Ackerman, A Natural
History of the Senses

thirty-nine:
head

When we are born, the top of the head is perhaps the most sensitive part of our bodies. Have you ever looked at a dog when you scratch the top of his/her head? They pull away and flinch— they don't like it at all.

Our head houses the seventh ("crown") chakra. It is said when the crown chakra is clear and open, it opens our own personal vortex into higher dimensions. It is also the point on our bodies that is closest to the sky, the place where "heaven" is for most of us.

My hair teaches me to protect and respect my head. My head is a sacred part of my body and the place which houses one of the most important organs we have: the brain.

forty: moisture

If I do nothing, I moisturize my hair. Every single day. My hair is super-duper dry and moisture keeps my hair from crackling into broken strands in my hands.

The body needs moisture, too. Both inside (the best form is water) and out. Moist skin, eyes and hair are a sign of good health and that everything is working together for good. Glow comes from moisture.

My hair teaches me the importance of hydrating: body mind and soul.

forty-one: protein

Hair is primarily comprised of protein—it is essential that we get enough of it internally in order for our bodies to function in an optimal fashion. Eggs, meat and fish are great forms of protein and— if you're a pescatarian like me—things like beans and tofu should be incorporated into your diet for a healthy, balanced constitution.

My hair teaches me to incorporate multiple forms of protein into my diet for a healthy mind and body.

forty-two: "i am not my hair"

Well, yes… and no. "I am not my hair" is a line of a song by the great songstress, Ms. India Arie. It is true that no one is simply their hair, a very small portion of our bodies. It is also true, however, that your hair is a part of you and should be treated with all the love, respect, nurture and care as every other part of you!

My hair teaches me that it **is** a part of me—my hair grows out of my head— but I am also more than the sum of my parts.

forty-three:
invest

I remember reading the book "Rich Dad, Poor Dad" several years ago. The "Rich Dad" became rich because he did one thing that "Poor Dad" never did—invest.

Investing doesn't always happen in the form of money. I believe education is a most valuable investment; time is another.

Investing in myself —and my hair—reminds me that I am valuable and I am worth nurturing. This kind of investment has yielded dividends I can scarcely express. Try it and you'll see what I mean.

My hair teaches me to invest in myself so that I may be able to invest in others.

forty-four: humility

"Nobody knows anything." A very successful writer, William Goldman, said this about Hollywood years ago. People still use this quote today because it holds true.

Well, it holds true in life outside of Hollywood, too. People can give you any manner of advice about this or that, share their hints, tips and techniques. For example, if you asked 100 happily married people what has made their marriage successful, you'll probably get 100 wildly different answers.

While there is merit in learning from those who have gone before, nobody really knows anything— they only know what has worked for them.

The same is true of this book, too! I FOUND GOD IN MY HAIR is my "take" on what I've learned about life via my relationship with my hair. It is my greatest wish that you find it valuable to your life.

At the same time, I know that my hair teaches me what monks have chanted for hundreds of years: "I know nothing."

"I'm talking about a little truth-in-packaging here. To be perfectly frank, you don't quite look like yourself. And if you walk around looking like someone other than who you are, you could end up getting the wrong job, the wrong friends, who knows what-all. You could end up with somebody else's life."

I shrugged again, and smiled. "This is my life," I said. "It doesn't seem like the wrong one."

— Michael Cunningham, A Home at
the End of the World

forty-five: begin

Nothing happens until you begin. Nothing. Most people talk about beginning long before they do; others never begin at all. Beginning any endeavor is the first sign that you are serious enough about it to take action. Beginning is a crucial first step to all things.

I live by the principle "what can be done today should be done today." This ideology usually keeps me up burning the candle at both ends, LOL! I never take for granted that I will wake up tomorrow. Because I just might not.

When I decided to wear my naturally textured hair, the first thing I did was cut off all my chemically relaxed hair. I didn't delay, mostly because I was eager to get to the other side. And I knew if I cut my hair now, the sooner I would get the results I wanted.

My hair teaches me the importance of beginning today. Right now!

forty-six: grow

The hair on our heads is similar to a plant; hair has three stages of evolution and the "growth" stage is the longest of them all.

It seemed like, after I did the "Big Chop," it took forever for my hair just to grow to my shoulders! There's little worse than trying to manage an in-between length for a long period of time. The number of available hairstyles is NOT limitless:)

My hair teaches me that growing is a sign of health and that growth of any kind is not without its pains.

NYPD BLUE (ABC)

Right after "24," I did a stint on NYPD Blue. I auditioned for this show about 12 times over several years before I actually got a role (the great June Lowry Johnson and her team cast me in this and several other shows, including TRUE BLOOD!). For all you actors out there: keep going and don't stop! Just because you audition and don't get the role, doesn't mean you won't get the next one. Or the next one or the next one...PERSISTENCE! :) One day, I was so sick of my hair, I decided to cut it all off–myself. This was the result. Everyone loved it, including me!

forty-seven: ask

"Ask and ye shall receive." Ever wonder why you're not getting what you want in life?

ARE YOU ASKING FOR IT?

It might sound simple, but you'd be astounded by the number of people walking the earth who simply never ask for what they want. Perhaps they don't want to sound pushy or arrogant. I tell you, I've felt this way in my life too. Over the years, though, I've learned that closed mouths don't get fed. I was a shy child in school who rarely raised her hand; now, I'm an actress. Public speaking has become one of my most favorite things to do. I can't shut up!

When I started on this hair odyssey, there was a lot I didn't know. When I started asking (and watching the ladies on Youtube and following hair bloggers), I didn't feel so alone and grew more confident.

My hair teaches me that asking is the primary way to get what I want. It is also the simplest!

"There's a reason why forty, fifty, and sixty don't look the way they used to, and it's not because of feminism, or better living through exercise. It's because of hair dye. In the 1950's only 7 percent of American women dyed their hair; today there are parts of Manhattan and Los Angeles where there are no gray-haired women at all."
— Nora Ephron

forty-eight: alone

I spend a great deal of time alone. I like it that way. I can hear my thoughts, commune with nature and create with the universe. My senior thesis was about a man named Henry David Thoreau and his "experiment" at Walden Pond, a log cabin in the middle of nowhere where he lived for two years—alone.

It was while I was alone that I got the inspiration to write this book!

My hair teaches me to never underestimate the value of quality time with myself, of being alone.

forty-nine: wisdom

"Wisdom is better than silver and gold." No truer words have ever been spoken! Wisdom teaches me to listen more than I speak; it has also taught me to adopt the practice of "smiling and nodding" whenever I hear someone say something outrageous or absurd. Sometimes things just ain't worth the effort or the brouhaha that will result in your putting in your two cents about it.

This book is about the wisdom I've learned—and earned— in dealing with a part of myself that has, for years, caused a great deal of frustration. But it was wisdom that encouraged me to create the space to consider another truth about my hair.

My hair teaches me that wisdom is the gateway to peace.

"Beware of her fair hair, for she excels all women in the magic of her locks; and when she winds them round a young man's neck, she will not ever set him free again."
— Johann Wolfgang von Goethe

fifty-two: spirit

s the ultimate muse. It is everywhere all the time,
ing us to our Ultimate Good. According to the
ary, it is "the vital principal in humans, animating
dy or mediating between body and soul."
kes practice to get in alignment with one's sprit,
en more practice to keep it there (usually in the
regular prayer and meditation).
ploring my relationship with my hair helps me to
gned with my purpose and my spirit.

fifty: power

This might sound trite, but getting control over my hair
made me feel very powerful; so powerful, in fact, I began
to cultivate the confidence that maybe—just maybe—I
had power over other areas of my life! The more I worked
on my hair, the more I was able to confront everything
else in my life I felt needed an overhaul.

My hair teaches me that Fear is really False Evidence
Appearing Real (F.E.A.R). I have power over every area
of my life all the time, despite how it looks.

"She was the most beautiful creature on Earth —
her hair said so in that language only hair can speak."
— Gabriel Bá, Daytripper

fifty-c
femini:

f

My mother had me when she wa
mom, she took on both roles in
for the lack of balance a woman
up in a household.

Because I had a mother wh
lot of growing up on my own—th
I had to figure out by myself. I
was young enough to work, and

There have been times in
a traditionally "masculine" role
slayer"—because I had to! Wh
hair, I accessed and unlocked

My hair helps me to emb
sweet power of femininity.

Spirit is
beckor
diction
the bo

It ta
and ev
form of

Ex
stay ali

Her father sagged as relief spread through him. "I thought something awful was happening." She frowned. "Something awful was happening. It could have got stuck in my hair."

— Derek Landy, Dark Days

fifty-three: help

Asking for help is both the most vulnerable and strongest action you can take on behalf of yourself.

Independence and self-sufficiency have been the hallmarks I have built my life on. But sometimes, being dependent and allowing others to do for you in times of need or crisis is very necessary to ensure your own survival. Sometimes, the best thing you can do is allow yourself to be carried along for a bit.

In times of crisis it is, interestingly enough, my hair that soothes me. I treat it with extra loving care, moisturizing and nurturing it. It helps me to feel calm so I can cultivate the confidence to ask for help when I need it.

BUTTERFLY RISING (W Movies)

My directorial debut, Butterfly Rising, is a movie about the town seductress and a grief stricken singer who take a road trip to meet a medicine man named Lazarus. I wore many hats on this movie: writer, director, producer and star. That's my character (Rose Johnson)— and yes, that's a weave (though my real hair wasn't much shorter than that). This is a scene with La'Reya Brown, a terrific young talent, who plays my daughter Grace. Butterfly Rising is perhaps my most significant, all-around artistic achievement thus far. It was inspired by the death of my brother; I also wrote the book of the same name.

fifty-four:
inspire

I was asked many years ago what I thought my purpose on the planet was. "I'd like to inspire others," I said. I think I was about 10 years old.

I often see the best in people when they can't see it for themselves. I hope my journey will inspire people to believe in their dreams, just like I hope this book will inspire people to think big and authentically be themselves.

My hair journey is one I hope will inspire others to live their true, authentic selves.

fifty-five: music

When I'm taking time with myself—with my hair— I often put on some music and dance around the house. If my hair were a song, I think it would be some jazz-like ditty—the Miles David kind. It's textured, complex and filled with riffs.

Music is a universal art form that transcends time, space and cultures; it unifies and soothes. You ever notice the number of people walking down the street with earphones these days? Almost everyone!

My hair helps me to enjoy and appreciate music. Music plays a soulful role in the undercurrent to my life.

"Naturally curly hair is a curse, and don't ever let anyone tell you different."

— Mary Ann Shaffer, The Guernsey Literary and Potato Peel Pie Society

fifty: power

This might sound trite, but getting control over my hair made me feel very powerful; so powerful, in fact, I began to cultivate the confidence that maybe—just maybe—I had power over other areas of my life! The more I worked on my hair, the more I was able to confront everything else in my life I felt needed an overhaul.

My hair teaches me that Fear is really False Evidence Appearing Real (F.E.A.R). I have power over every area of my life all the time, despite how it looks.

"She was the most beautiful creature on Earth —
her hair said so in that language only hair can speak."
— Gabriel Bá, Daytripper

Her father sagged as relief spread through him. "I thought something awful was happening." She frowned. "Something awful was happening. It could have got stuck in my hair."

— Derek Landy, Dark Days

fifty-three: help

Asking for help is both the most vulnerable and strongest action you can take on behalf of yourself.

Independence and self-sufficiency have been the hallmarks I have built my life on. But sometimes, being dependent and allowing others to do for you in times of need or crisis is very necessary to ensure your own survival. Sometimes, the best thing you can do is allow yourself to be carried along for a bit.

In times of crisis it is, interestingly enough, my hair that soothes me. I treat it with extra loving care, moisturizing and nurturing it. It helps me to feel calm so I can cultivate the confidence to ask for help when I need it.

fifty-one: femininity

My mother had me when she was 15 years old. A single mom, she took on both roles in the house to make up for the lack of balance a woman and man ideally make up in a household.

Because I had a mother who was so young, I did a lot of growing up on my own—there were a lot of things I had to figure out by myself. I have had a job since I was young enough to work, and haven't stopped since.

There have been times in my life where I took on a traditionally "masculine" role— I call it the "dragon slayer"—because I had to! When I began to nurture my hair, I accessed and unlocked a feminine quality I enjoy.

My hair helps me to embrace and appreciate the sweet power of femininity.

fifty-two: spirit

Spirit is the ultimate muse. It is everywhere all the time, beckoning us to our Ultimate Good. According to the dictionary, it is "the vital principal in humans, animating the body or mediating between body and soul."

It takes practice to get in alignment with one's sprit, and even more practice to keep it there (usually in the form of regular prayer and meditation).

Exploring my relationship with my hair helps me to stay aligned with my purpose and my spirit.

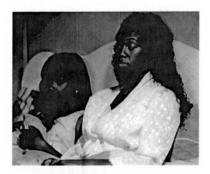

BUTTERFLY RISING (W Movies)

My directorial debut, Butterfly Rising, is a movie about the town seductress and a grief stricken singer who take a road trip to meet a medicine man named Lazarus. I wore many hats on this movie: writer, director, producer and star. That's my character (Rose Johnson)— and yes, that's a weave (though my real hair wasn't much shorter than that). This is a scene with La'Reya Brown, a terrific young talent, who plays my daughter Grace. Butterfly Rising is perhaps my most significant, all-around artistic achievement thus far. It was inspired by the death of my brother; I also wrote the book of the same name.

fifty-four:
inspire

I was asked many years ago what I thought my purpose on the planet was. "I'd like to inspire others," I said. I think I was about 10 years old.

I often see the best in people when they can't see it for themselves. I hope my journey will inspire people to believe in their dreams, just like I hope this book will inspire people to think big and authentically be themselves.

My hair journey is one I hope will inspire others to live their true, authentic selves.

fifty-six: mixed

In NYC, there is no dearth of mixed couples resulting in mixed-race babies. In addition to the Black/white blends, there are other mixes in Caribbean, African-American, Latin and Asian cultures.

There was a couple (the mom was White and the dad was Black) walking down the street with their daughter (she was about 3). I saw them staring at me for a long, long while. The man whispered something to the woman; she walked up to me.

"Excuse me," she said. "I hope you're not offended, but can you tell me what you use on your hair?" She gestured to her daughter's springy, dry curls. I was happy to oblige. Dad smiled, grateful and relieved.

There was a picture floating around Facebook a year or so ago about a white man joyfully braiding his mixed daughter's hair. It was a very popular picture! I remember "liking" it myself.

If you know a mixed couple who has a baby, lend 'em a hand! They might not know how to ask for help in fear they will say the wrong thing to the wrong person.

My hair helps me to have compassion for people who are mixed and makes me want to help them.

"Some of the worst mistakes in my life were haircuts."

— Jim Morrison

fifty-seven: friendship

For years, I regarded my hair as the Ultimate Enemy, a beast that needed to be tamed and subdued.

Now? My hair is my friend:)

fifty-eight: shrinkage

Textured hair is prone to shrinkage! It's easy to go from shoulder length to an afro as quick as a drop of water. It's a frustrating fact of having naturally textured hair.

In my early days as an actress, I remembered using the term "shrinkage" a lot as it related to my bank account, LOL! It was prone to shrinkage, too. But, just like hair, things can and do expand.

My hair teaches me that both shrinkage and expansion are natural parts of life.

"The worse the haircut, the better the man."

— John Green

fifty-nine: leave it alone

Have you ever waited for money in the mail and made the comings and goings of your mailman/woman your sole obsession? Every hear of the adage "a watched pot never boils?" It seems like, when you need or want something and you know it's on its way, it takes forever to reach you. But It only seems that way 'cause you're fixated on it.

I use to fiddle with my hair constantly. In order to achieve the hair results I wanted, I realized I had to leave it alone! Whenever I get antsy about something, I find it best to transfer my attention to something more productive. Dancing, writing, working out—some physical activity— almost always does the trick and relaxes me in the end.

My hair teaches me there is value to simply leaving well enough alone.

sixty:
less is more

When you're trying something new, it's tempting to over-indulge. For example, when I decided to wear my naturally textured hair, I tried just about every hair product on the market! My bathroom was covered in potions and bottles all designed to make my hair longer, healthier, shinier. I was using so much product it began building up on my hair and white beads started to form.

Now, I have a few hair products that are tried and true—stuff I make, so I know it works. I don't need a million-and-one products to get the desired results, just a select few with high quality ingredients and high-performance qualities. I'm happier, my hair's happier and my purse is happier, too!

My hair teaches me that, in most instances, less is definitely more.

TRUE BLOOD (HBO)

Now, Little Miss Kenya has had a few looks on True Blood! Here's the splendid array: (1-left) what I call the 'snatch back' (2-right) I decided to give her a little flair and gave her a bang. She's a no-nonsense gal, and I thought this look would soften her a bit:) (3-below) here I am in all my textured glory! It was around this time I started to really take stock of my hair, what I was doing with it and what made me really, truly happy. Since I played a cop on True Blood, I thought the producers would make me pull my hair back–but they didn't! The only comment I got was: "your hair looks nice."

TRUE BLOOD (HBO)

sixty-one: light

Light is the source of good. Naturally curly hair does not reflect light easily; healthy, shiny hair reflects light like nothing else.

Light has always been a sure sign to me that I am on the right path, that I'm going the right way. Wherever there is light, I know that the truth will be illuminated.

My hair teaches me that light always lights the way.

"I cut my hair so it looks like I just woke up all the time, so that I can be like, what year is it? I've been asleep since the 80s."

— Jarod Kintz, A Story That Talks about Talking Is Like Chatter to Chattering Teeth, and Every Set of Dentures Can Attest to the Fact That No…

sixty-two:
transparency

Did you know that white—or "gray" hair is not really white or gray in color but is actually transparent? Older and wiser hair is simply no more than a lack of pigment.

Being transparent in one's life is a sign of extreme health. It tells the world you're honest, trustworthy and creates a sense of safety, openness and inclusion that harboring secrets will never do. Secrets can inspire fear and requires clandestine energy to keep the truth from ever reaching the light of day.

There's a time for keeping quiet and there's a time for transparency. My hair teaches me that being transparent is nothing to be afraid of and that it helps to keep me connected to others.

sixty-three:
journey

Life is a journey. It is said that arriving at a destination has none of the joys of actually traveling there.

It's easy to get so focused on arriving at the destination–a goal– that we neglect to see the blessings along the way or even the revelations that the prayers we were praying have already been answered!

Discovering this new relationship with my hair has helped me to embrace other changes in my life with greater ease, making the journey of "getting there" feel a lot less rocky.

My hair teaches me that the "juice" is most often in the journey, not the destination.

sixty-four: judgment

In many areas of our society, there seems to be a lot of judgment concerning hairstyles: are you a 1B or a 4C on the hair texture chart? Do you wear your hair straight? Relaxed? Dreads? Braids?

If the need to judge others were removed from the human psyche, I truly believe that people would enjoy more peace within themselves and be happier and kinder to one another.

My hair teaches me that there is beauty in the fact that we all have the right to make personal choices regarding our lives. It also helps me to respect other people's choices that are different from my own.

"Long hair will send you to hell!"
— Hidekaz Himaruya, Hetalia: Axis Powers, Vol. 2

sixty-five:
insecurity

Whether you wear your naturally textured hair, sport braids, decide to get your hair relaxed, blow it straight, get a weave, etc. the world will, undoubtedly, have opinions. Other people's thoughts about how you should live your life may make you feel unstable and insecure.

When you're feeling this way, it could be a great time to check out from people who want you to conform to their reality and check in with people who celebrate your self-expression and encourage your uniqueness!

At the end of the day, your decisions regarding your life are yours and yours alone to make—as long as they don't hurt others.

My hair teaches me to fortify myself when I feel insecure.

sixty-six:
reverence

According to the dictionary, reverence is defined as "a feeling or attitude of deep respect tinged with awe." An attitude of reverence towards life is helpful, even —and especially—when life gives you lemons.

That's the time to make lemonade and have reverence toward the Circle of Life!

I am constantly awe-inspired by the human body: to heal itself, a woman's ability to conceive and bear children, the goose bumps we get when danger looms nearby. Our hair is one of the many outward and perfect manifestations of the work our body does 24 hours a day, 7 days a week 365 days a year.

My hair teaches me to have reverence for everything inside me and around me.

"A few other couples joined us on the dance floor and we lost ourselves among them. I'd never been able to figure out exactly what was involved in slow dancing, so I contented myself, as I had since high school, with gripping my partner to me, letting out awkward breaths against her ear, and tipping from foot to foot like someone waiting for a bus. I could feel the sweat cooling on her forearms and smell a trace of apples in her hair."

— Michael Chabon, Wonder Boys

sixty-seven:
study

I love to learn new things, especially ones related to my field. I don't profess to be an expert in, say, technology but I try to be aware of what tools are out there that can help me be a better storyteller and connect to people.

When I decided to wear my naturally textured hair, I did a lot of study on the subject— I read books, blogs, did research. Study sharpens my mind, increases opportunities and helps me to realize how many options already exist.

It also reinforces the old adage that everything you need to know is in a book:)

My hair teaches me that my mind is a great sponge for information. Study helps to keep my mind active, sharp and current.

ORANGE IS THE NEW BLACK (Netflix)

Here we are today: the most interesting, textured role I've ever been asked–and given the privilege–to play. Crystal Burset is in a very complicated relationship with her transgendered spouse, Sophia Burset (played by Laverne Cox). Interestingly–and coincidentally–Crystal and Sophia are hairstylists on the show and own a hair salon together! The incomparable Jodie Foster directed this, the third episode of season 1.

ORANGE IS THE NEW BLACK (Netflix)

sixty-eight: new

"Out with the old, in with the new" is an adage that holds true. Sometimes, it's best to sweep things out in order to make space for the new.

Other times, when "new" arrives, it's so appealing and wonderful you didn't even know you needed it! It's like finding a glass of water in the desert and not realizing you were thirsty. "New" can feel like a friend you had always been waiting for.

I wash my hair every few weeks—some say that's a long while, but if you have naturally textured hair, it's really just right. Washing everything away and starting afresh is healthy, especially if you're using shampoos/conditioners with silicones (which are not water soluble and you'll need shampoo to get out completely). Also, by not allowing moistures and butters to penetrate the strands, your hair is more prone to breakage.

My hair teaches me the importance of starting afresh—starting anew—every day.

I've seen knives pierce the chest,
Children dying in the road
Crawling things hooked and baited,
Rapists bound and then castrated,
Villains singed in public square.
Yet none these sights did make me cringe
Like when my Love cut all her hair.

— Roman Payne

sixty-nine: gentle

I'm a native New Yorker and we're not known for being the gentlest folks in the world— but we get stuff done. New Yorkers always seem as if they're rushing to or from someplace very important—someplace other than where they are right now.

Taking the time to be gentle—with myself and others— seems like a departure from my busy and often hectic life, but without gentleness, I'd probably be just a bag of nerves plowing through this or that, knocking things down, making tons of mistakes and hurting feelings along the way.

Taking the time to be gentle with your hair requires a lot of patience! When I was thinking about wearing my naturally textured hair, I watched a ton of videos on YouTube. They all recommended conditioning your hair—sopping wet—in the shower. Now, when your hair is curly like mine, the desire to want to rake the comb through from roots to tips is very, very strong. But I learned the hard way that it did nothing but rip that new

growth I worked so hard for out of my head as I watched it fall down the drain...

My hair teaches me to slow down and be gentle, especially when I have the urge to go fast.

seventy: pride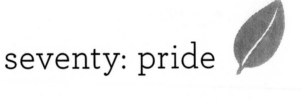

One of the seven deadly sins, pride keeps us from getting the assistance we need. It also puts us in a place of expectation when we feel those whom we've helped in the past owes us something.

"Pride goeth before the fall." I know some people who would sooner die than admit defeat, chart a new course or simply apologize. Their chests are usually puffed out so much they can hardly breathe. Their stoicism renders them wooden and immoveable, like emotionless non-humans.

The "good" pride, though, can have you swinging your locks from side to side, beaming from the inside out from the swell you feel from wearing your hair in whatever style you like. Feeling good about yourself always engenders positive pride.

My hair teaches me to discern when I'm feeling prideful.

seventy-one:
fall down

We all fall down. Physically and metaphorically—it happens. Everything never goes all right for all of us all the time. The important thing, though, is what you're doing while you're in the Valley of Life.

Look around while you're down in the Valley. There are jewels there! Gifts wrapped in unpleasant-ness. It's up to you to make sure you learn the lessons life is trying to teach you so that, when it's time to get back up, you don't have to return to the Valley again. If you're wondering why certain circumstances in your life keep recurring, it's because you haven't learned the lesson. Ask questions of your pain: you are the only one with the antidote.

You've been down around your feet too long. Get up and dust yourself off! Nurture yourself—this time, start with your hair.

"What's outside my head and what's inside my head aren't worth mentioning. What's worth mentioning is what's on my head – my hair. Whatever happens, I'll still be as fashionably coiffed as I was before the war broke out and I got dementia."

— Bauvard, Evergreens Are Prudish

seventy-two:
dream

The idea for I FOUND GOD IN MY HAIR began when I dreamed a perfect world for myself. I had just come through a personally devastating time— and things seemed to be looking up— but I was cautious, gob-smacked from being Down in the Valley for so long. It was in my dreams where this collection of essays was born, from the single thought: "if I can get control of my hair, I can get control of my life."

My hair teaches me that dreams can be made real with hard work, dedication and faith. Plus, I get by with a (lotta) help from my friends, family. And God:)

seventy-three: slip

My hair can get pretty unruly pretty quickly, and I've learned that conditioners with loads of slip are the ones that work best for me. Slip is the degree to which hair products "slip" down your hair shaft. Products with lots of slip tend to help untangle naturally textured hair more easily.

In life, sometimes it's best to let comments or circumstances roll right off your back. "Don't take things personally" comes from one of my favorite books, The Four Agreements. If you let things roll off your back like water to a duck, they'll have less of a chance of staying with you, taking root and causing you unhappiness.

My hair teaches me that, sometimes letting "slip" do the work is better than pushing an undesirable person, thing or circumstance away. You also save energy that way. Let it slip away on its own...

seventy-four:
type

There's a lot of brouhaha about hair type, the system that puts different hair textures into different "categories." For example, a 1B's hair tends toward straight while a 4C tends toward kinky. My thought is that this system was created to make things easier for people to identify the best products for their hair. Others say it creates "hierarchy" and should be eliminated.

I have a busy life, so if someone has thought of a system to make buying hair products easy-breezy, then I'm all about it! At the same time, I can dig not wanting to be put in a "box." In fact, there are some heads of hair that fall under multiple hair types.

My hair teaches me not to sweat "categories." We're all in one, whether we like it or not. I also know that no one of us is exactly like the other, and that we are all unique and individually special.

"Long hair will make thee look dreadfully to thine enemies, and manly to thy friends: it is, in peace, an ornament; in war, a strong helmet; it...deadens the leaden thump of a bullet: in winter, it is a warm nightcap; in summer, a cooling fan of feathers."

— Thomas Dekker,
The Guls Horne Booke, 1609

seventy-five: home

Home is where the heart is—it is also where your bed is, your food is, your family/children are. For most of us, home is where we replenish, nourish, rest and enjoy others.

For me, home is a lot more than that: it's my sanctuary. It is the place where I write, dream and create. It is the safest place in the world, the place I love the most. I love spending evenings in the quiet of my home with a hot oil treatment or a deep conditioner on my hair and hanging with my pooch, Macarena.

My hair teaches me that home is where the hair is.

seventy-six:
thank you

Earlier, we talked about gratitude, which is more a "feeling" of thankfulness. Saying the words "thank you," however, is the ACT of acknowledging that you have received something of value. 'Thank you' is gratitude in action, your show of sign that you appreciate something.

Jimmy Fallon has made a joke of writing 'Thank You' notes on his late night show. Although it's a humorous segment, he's doing something very powerful here; I read a study that showed if you thanked someone for something they gave you in a timely fashion, they are 84% more likely to give to you again.

Who knew two little words could be so powerful?

My hair teaches me that saying the words "thank you" make others feel valued and helps me remember to do work that creates value in the lives of others. Because, the truth is, it is better to give than to receive. And none of us gets anything done alone.

"The night crackled…everything had turned to static electricity in the heat. I combed my hair to watch the sparks fly from the ends."

— Janet Fitch, White Oleander

seventy-seven: deep

I have always listened beneath the words when people speak; body movements, hand gestures—even moments of silence—speak volumes about what a person is really thinking and feeling. This probably has a lot to do with me being an actress; I'm kind of obsessed to learn and explore why people do the things that they do. We are always telegraphing to the world who we are, whether we're aware of it or not.

Some who have read this book have called it "deep." Who knew you could learn so much about life from some strands atop your head?

My hair teaches me that going deep beneath the surface of things is where I find gold.

HAIRiette OF HARLEM

Know this girl? Just call her..."HAIRiette"! For more, on HAIRiette and her hair, check out Hairiette.com. You'll be glad you did:)

seventy-eight: create

Creation is the one ability humans have over any other species—it is, in my view, the most powerful gift given us by God. Human beings have used this gift of creation to make bombs, computers and even light bulbs. The privilege of creating gives us both the vast ability to make something that can either inspire and uplift others or completely annihilate them.

Our hair is an extraordinary canvas to create who we are, how we see the world, if and how we take care of ourselves. It is often the first and most obvious point of reference most people have of one another since our hair is just above our faces.

My hair teaches me that the ability to create is a gift. I honor and respect this gift, and I choose to use it in a way that helps others.

seventy-nine:
money

Like it or not, money is necessary—though I have spent gobs of time imagining a world where it was not. The concept of money seems to be elusive to some, but others (Bill Gates! Warren Buffett!) seem to have mastered the art of making it like few others.

From all the research I've done on the subject, money is simply the result of spiritual energy, no more and no less. It works no different from anything else in the world you "want." You must be the change you want to see. If you want money, then you must give it.

But you don't need a lot of it to get healthy hair! Along with a shampoo, you know what I use in my hair? My own mixes Shea butter, olive and coconut oil—a friend bought me some baobab oil from Africa (known as the 'Tree of Life') and I love it! These are all natural, high quality ingredients that work great on naturally textured hair for enormous value.

My hair teaches me that we all have equal ability to have as much money as we want and that it costs very little to have the things you need most in life that give you the greatest joy.

"Red hair, sir, in my opinion, is dangerous."
— P.G. Wodehouse, Very Good, Jeeves!

eighty: plan

It is said "God laughs at our plans." It is also true that many people fail without them.

When I made my first film, Butterfly Rising, I did not have a plan—I simply wanted to make a movie without having an idea of how it was going to be marketed or distributed. I learned a lot through the process, so that I was able to plan for my next project in a very different fashion. I've heard some very successful people say they never planned for their good fortune, and I've heard others who are just as successful say they plan for absolutely everything.

I believe in a good plan; I also believe a plan can and should be revised as you get new information—sometimes even thrown own completely.

My hair teaches me that, every day when I get up, my hair has a plan. And sometimes, it just ain't mine:)

eighty-one: productive

Staying focused when there's a lot going on can be tough. For some, it's easy to stray off course and for others, that's when their focus really intensifies.

When I'm tired and getting home from a late night out, sometimes all I want to do is crawl into bed without doing my nightly conditioning routine, which is how my hair's gone from a hot mess to pretty good!

My hair teaches me that being productive—even when I don't feel like it— helps me to stay on course and reach my goals.

"It was an odd situation. For a century and a half, men got rid of their own hair, which was perfectly comfortable, and instead covered their heads with something foreign and uncomfortable. Very often it was actually their own hair made into a wig. People who couldn't afford wigs tried to make their hair look like a wig."

— Bill Bryson, At Home:
A Short History of Private Life

eighty-two:
stress

Stress is something we all experience; some are better at handling it than others. Still, there are some people who take the most stressful situations in their lives and turn them into their biggest assets.

I try to keep stress at a minimum. I live a very simple private life (my business life is far more complicated). Things like walking my dog, exercising and disconnecting (I find having access to my phone and getting/receiving e-mails 24 hours a day, 7 days a week to be terribly stressful) really help. I take great pains to turn off my phone so I'm not tempted to look and take some quiet time with myself once every day.

Stress has also been known to wreak havoc on the tresses! A friend's hair fell out in clumps recently due to the toll she was taking on her body, mind and soul.

My hair teaches me that stress is a natural part of life, but there are things I can do to help me manage it.

"What's outside my head and what's inside my head aren't worth mentioning. What's worth mentioning is what's on my head – my hair. Whatever happens, I'll still be as fashionably coiffed as I was before the war broke out and I got dementia."

— Bauvard, Evergreens Are Prudish

eighty-three:
accident

I am not very fond of the words "mistake" or "accident." Granted, we all make them from time to time, but I think they're only costly when you don't learn from them. Also, sometimes a "mistake" just means you didn't do what you set out to do originally. For example, making penicillin was a "mistake" Alexander Fleming made back in the early 1900's. It was a happy "accident" that would cure millions of people around the world and keep even millions more alive.

I've tried countless hair regimes since I started on this journey— I've learned what works best for my hair mostly is the simple stuff I make by hand. My experience has been there are no real shortcuts in life. I learned a lot about my hair—what it needs, what it doesn't like— by making tons of "mistakes."

My hair teaches me that life is full of opportunities for "happy accidents" and that, whenever I veer off course, I may not be going the "wrong" way after all.

"Whatever the reason, first place was always Solo, always, always, always, and second place was usually Chewbacca, because if you weren't the one saving the galaxy, you might as well be eight feet tall and covered with hair."

— Charles Yu, How to Live Safely in a Science Fictional Universe

eighty-four:
living

The personal computer was created so that we could get things done easier, faster, more efficiently and spend more time living, enjoying our friends and family. Instead, we've become zombies, ears plugged up, eyes glazed and glued to big screens like the ones on our computers and the small ones, like our phones.

I've seen some folks on the hair journey get downright obsessive about it. Their rituals, potions—well, they're just not enjoying life at all. The truth is, taking care of yourself—via your hair or any other part of your body— should really only enhance your life.

My hair teaches me that I can live better, healthier and wiser.

eighty-five: normal

I believe this is a word that should be stricken from the English language. What does it mean, really? That each of us should look, talk, walk and be like everyone else? How does this make the world go round? Is "normal' something that we should really be striving for?

Life is infinitely more interesting in the "abnormal" world. The truth is, isn't it normal to know that we are all abnormal in some way?

There is no "normal" hair type or style. I wore my hair in the ways I had seen others wear theirs because I didn't want to seem abnormal or different. Can you believe that?

My hair teaches me it's normal and good and right that we're all hopelessly, beautifully abnormal.

My hair today in its naturally textured state:
strong healthy and shiny.

eighty-six: free

There are two expressions I live by: "everything free ain't cheap" and "the best things in life are free." I believe both are true and that the expressions are not opposites, but rather they complement each other.

The thing is, we've got to be able to discern what it is to be "free." I'm amazed at how people can take something just because it's free even when they don't like it or will never use it. "Well, it was free." I am also equally astounded by folks who will use things of an inferior quality just because they're free.

I've got a ton of useless hair products I got for free that, if I used them, they'd end up costing me quite a lot because of their inferior ingredients. At the same time, the superior ingredients I use for my hair concoctions are plentiful and have great value. Go figure!

My hair teaches me that "free" things sometimes require further inspection and that they might cost more than they're worth.

"I won't fall in love," he said, "I swear,"
As he ran his fingers through her hair.
She smiled because she knew he was wrong.
It wouldn't take long."

— Evette Carter

eighty-seven: family

Most African-American families are a veritable rainbow of colors and hair textures. I'm brown skinned with curly hair; my sister has green eyes and wears dreadlocks. My mom's folks are from the islands (Jamaica) and my dad's are from the South (Georgia). And yes, my sister and I have the same parents.

My hair teaches me to embrace the wonderful physical differences in my own backyard in the form of my family.

eighty-eight: feet

We've been spending a lot of time talking about the very top of our bodies— but what about the bottom? Your feet support you all day, every day. It's my view they deserve the same amount of love and attention as your hair and head! I suspect most of us take our feet for granted, but really, we should honor them.

I know that when my hair is done and I have on a good pair of shoes, I feel great. A good pair of shoes was so important to Conrad Cantzen that, in 1945, he bequeathed his estate to The Actor's Fund with the stipulation that it should be used to help actors purchase shoes so they did not appear "down at the heels" when auditioning.

My hair teaches me that my feet do some pretty heavy lifting and that the bottom is just as important as the top.

eighty-nine: smarter not harder

People who know me know I am a hard worker: I am determined and can be quite focused, especially when I put my mind to achieving a goal.

Over time, I began to realize that sometimes it's more effective to work smarter—not harder. Working smarter makes things more efficient. Delegation of duties is smart (I've come to know that division of labor is far better for a project than taking on everything myself). I'm not a control freak, but I've been disappointed by folks in the past and it hurts. I've long held the adage, "if you want to get something done, best to do it yourself."

Well, I've realized its actually better to have someone else do the things you don't do as well. I love it when I'm the person in the room who knows the least. It's inspiring and there's just so much to learn!

Same thing with my hair. Over time, I've developed a simple routine for myself based on this concept—one product can be 10 times more effective than 50 products. My hair teaches me that working smarter–not harder–is the preferred route to achieving my goals.

ninety: best

What does it mean to be "the best?" Well, I think it's relative. Who's to say an actress who wins an Academy Award is better than any of the other lovely—and equally talented—ladies in her category? Recently, I had the task of evaluating students for scholarships to independent schools across the country. There were only 30 slots and 84 applicants. Now, the truth is, there were about 45 applicants who were qualified—equally smart and talented—but there just weren't enough slots for all of them. Who gets in and who doesn't? It came down to splitting hairs. I left that day in a heap of tears with the knowledge that some very deserving students would leave without this life-changing opportunity only because of a number, and no other reason. Life seemed terribly unfair in that moment, but I was heartened by the fact that, if these students were willing, other opportunities would reveal themselves—or, even better, they would create ones on their own.

There has been a lot of talk about hair being "good" or "bad," particularly in the African-American community. I think it's pretty disgusting, but I digress—as I said earlier, this collection of essays is NOT about the socio-political manifestations of hair. Whatever you do or whomever you are, it's important that you be and act your best.

My hair teaches me to be the best that I can and resist the urge to compare myself to others.

ninety-one: animals

I love animals! In my first film, Butterfly Rising, you meet my dog, Macarena. Macarena is a Black Lab I "rescued" (though sometimes I think: did she really rescue me?) shortly after my brother died. Nine years later, she looks significantly older (those gray hairs and white eyebrows!) but there's no lack of pep in her step.

Most animals are covered in hair in abundance—affectionately known as fur. I sometimes call Macarena "My Fur Baby!" Petting her body—her fur— gives me a sense of peace and contentment. Studies show that people who have animals—and pet them—have lower blood pressure, are healthier and tend to be happier.

My dog teaches me that an abundance of hair is a good thing. Especially when it's on the body of a four-legged being whose only goal in life is to see you happy and give you love. That's the best!

"It was a smooth silvery voice that matched her hair. It had a tiny tinkle in it, like bells in a doll's house. I thought that was silly as soon as I thought of it."
— Raymond Chandler, The Big Sleep

ninety-two: time

Time is the one thing in our lives we can never get back. Time is always going forward. People like to sleep in abundance after they've "lost" it but, the truth is, it can never be made up! Time stands still for no one. It does not discriminate and marches to the beat of the clock. I have come to respect time. It's one of the few things in life you have no control over, so why not go with it?

In order for anything to change—including the condition of your hair—it will take time.

My hair teaches me that time is something no one can hasten and that it's best to work with it and not against it.

ninety-three: present

I am a firm believer in the idea that the present is a gift. We tend to take the present for granted, always examining the past (and having regrets which are a colossal waste of time) or jutting into the unknown, the future. The truth is, it is only now—the present—where you have the opportunity to forgive the faults of the past and lay the foundation to create the future you imagine.

My hair teaches me that time is a gift and, in it, are the thoughts I plant like seeds to create the life of my dreams.

ninety-four: color

I love color! Whenever I move into a new home, I paint each room a color I am inspired by. Right now, my bedroom is blue (like the sea); at the window are white, billowy curtains that remind me of the clouds. I wanted my bedroom to feel like the sky—with all its space and time—and I achieved that feeling with those two colors.

Aside from tattoos, what other part of your body can you color except your hair? I've seen pink, green and blue hair. I've even seen tiger-striped and cougar spotted manes! If there is a color you can dream of, it can be had—and put on your hair. Personally, I'm partial to ingredients that are gonna be gentle on my hair. Henna is a great, natural alternative.

My hair teaches me that color can add a bit of spice to my life and helps me to express who I am and create the person I want the world to see.

ninety-five: flow

I love the water. There is a natural ebb and flow to everything. "Flow" has been very noticeable in the form of my relationships: sometimes it's necessary that one gives more than the other— and vice versa, depending on the needs of life at the time.

I've learned that, whenever I go against the 'flow,' things rarely turn out the way I'd like them to go. It reminds me of the Rolling Stones song "you can't always get what you want... you get what you need!" Flow always gives me what I need, not necessarily what I want when I want it. Flow is dictated by the soul —which, I believe, is always in charge—and not the personality.

Years ago, I decided I wanted to be a writer—but then I got an acting job. And then I got another acting job and then another... I went with the "flow," still writing all the while with the faith that, eventually, writing would merge with acting and the two would flow together. I didn't know how or when, I just knew that it would.

Also, when I decided to go *with* my hair (instead of against it), I began to see how that simple decision led to an in-flow of creative thoughts and ideas.

My hair teaches me to look for the "flow"—even if it's not the route I originally wanted to go–to help me reach my destination.

ninety-six: movement

I dance for exactly 10 minutes every day—alone—in my home. Movement gives me something equally as important as meditation. My blood circulates 'cause my heart is pumping, my skin—the largest organ in our bodies—starts to sweat and trapped energy gets dispersed.

When I was a little girl, I desperately wanted to have my hair hot combed. I had seen it done on everyone I knew around me, and I felt like I was missing out. My mother said she would not press my hair. So, one day, I went to my bedroom and loaded my hair with grease so that I could get the straight look that everyone else had. My hair was just a mass of thin, stingy strands with no movement whatsoever.

My hair teaches me the importance of movement in my life. And that there are many ways to get it (and I didn't need a whole heap 'o grease!)

"A few other couples joined us on the dance floor and we lost ourselves among them. I'd never been able to figure out exactly what was involved in slow dancing, so I contented myself, as I had since high school, with gripping my partner to me, letting out awkward breaths against her ear, and tipping from foot to foot like some-one waiting for a bus. I could feel the sweat cooling on her forearms and smell a trace of apples in her hair."

— Michael Chabon, Wonder Boys

ninety-seven: illness

While I was writing this collection of essays, I thought about the women (and men!) who had no hair due to auto-immune disorders like alopecia and illnesses like cancer. A dear friend was recently put into remission from brain cancer. How would she respond to a book about hair?

But, that's just it. This isn't a collection of essays book about "hair," per se; hair is the metaphor God gave me to get to the other side of Grace. God gives us all things—different struggles, battles to overcome—in hopes that we may come through a better, wiser, stronger and more vulnerable person. The truth is, you can put just about any word you want to fill in the sentence "I Found God in My_____."

My relationship with my hair is symbolic of many things but, most importantly, it was the device used to get to the other side of Grace.

ninety-eight: opportunity

I believe opportunity is revealing itself to us every moment of the day. If you pray for something, you may get it immediately: but are you in a space to receive it? Are you looking ahead—or behind you? Or worse, is your head hanging too low to the ground?

I have learned to be inspired by everything—"good" and "bad"— and see it all as an opportunity. An opportunity to grow. To meet new people. To have another experience. To share. To receive. To change my mind. To love. To give. To be.

My hair taught me that life is a treasure trove of endless opportunities.

What will you do with yours today?

epilogue

This collection of essays was written with a full and open heart. If you've received some inspiration from them (or even if you didn't, LOL!), I'd love to hear from you! Come visit me at hairiette.com

Keep Rising!

xo Tanya

NEW BOOK

MAR 1 6 2016

CPSIA information can be obtained at www.ICGtesting.com
Printed in the USA
LVOW10s1622160116

470957LV00001B/31/P